PACEMAKER®

Skills for Independent Living

WORKBOOK

Globe
Fearon

An imprint of Pearson Learning
Parsippany, New Jersey
www.pearsonlearning.com

Executive Editor: Eleanor Ripp
Lead Editor: Brian Hawkes
Lead Designer: April Okano
Cover Designer: Tricia Battipede
Production Editor: Debi Schlott
Electronic Specialist: Leslie Greenberg
Manufacturing Manager: Mark Cirillo

About the Cover: People need many skills to successfully live on their own. The images on the cover represent a variety of these skills. "To Do" lists help people organize themselves. People's keys open their apartments, houses, and cars. Smart and healthful shopping help people buy what they need. Bus and train schedules help people get to places on time. Finally, people need to earn money and stay on a budget. What are some other skills for independent living that people need? How could these skills be represented?

Pacemaker® Skills for Independent Living, Second Edition

Copyright © 2002 by Pearson Education, Inc., publishing as Globe Fearon, 299 Jefferson Road, Parsippany, New Jersey, 07054. All rights reserved. No part of this book may be reproduced or transmitted in any form or by any means, electronic, photographic, mechanical, or otherwise, including photocopying, recording, or by any information storage and retrieval system, without permission in writing from the publisher.

ISBN: 0-130-23825-2

Printed in the United States of America
1 2 3 4 5 6 7 8 9 10   05 04 03 02 01

GLOBE FEARON
An imprint of Pearson Learning
Parsippany, New Jersey
www.pearsonlearning.com
1-800-321-3106

Contents

A Note to the Student

Use this Workbook along with your *Pacemaker® Skills for Independent Living* textbook. The exercises in this Workbook are linked to the textbook lessons. This Workbook will help you do two things—practice and think critically. Look at the top of each exercise page. You will see that the exercise is labeled as either "Practice" or "Critical Thinking."

The "Practice" activities give you the opportunity to practice the skills you have learned in your textbook. These activities are similar to many of the activities in your textbook. The more you practice, the more you will remember. Set goals for yourself, and try to meet them as you do each set of exercises. Practice helps you master skills and leads to success on tests, in schoolwork, on the job, and in life.

The "Critical Thinking" activities will challenge you to think beyond what you have learned in your textbook. Critical thinking—or to put it another way, thinking critically—means putting information to use. For example, in your textbook, you will learn about eating healthy foods. A "Critical Thinking" activity in this Workbook then asks you to create a healthy food plan for yourself. You are applying the information you learned in your textbook to your own life.

This Workbook is a wonderful source of knowledge. By completing the activities, you will learn a great deal about life skills. The real value of this information will come when you are successfully living on your own.

1 ▶ Considering Qualities

Skills 1.1–1.3

Exercise 1

Practice

Read the situation below. Then answer the questions.

> Juan thought fishing was boring, but his dad loved to fish. Juan's 16th birthday was two weeks away. His father said, "I have a great idea, Juan. For your birthday, why don't we spend the whole weekend fishing, just you and me. That sounds great, doesn't it?"
>
> Juan did not know what to say. Two of the qualities that were most important to him were honesty and concern for others. He had to decide what to do.

1. If honesty is the most important quality to Juan, what might he say to his father?

_____

_____

_____

2. If concern for others is the most important quality to Juan, what might he say to his father?

_____

_____

_____

3. If you were Juan, what might you say to your father?

_____

_____

_____

4. What are some times when you might be tempted to be less than honest?

_____

_____

_____

Pacemaker® Skills for Independent Living   Copyright © by Pearson Education, Inc., publishing as Globe Fearon. All rights reserved.

1 ▶ Sorting Out Choices

Skills 1.2–1.4

Exercise 2

Critical Thinking

**Read the following situation to help Tanya make a wise decision.
Then think about Tanya's choices and their possible results. Write
your comments on the lines.**

> Tanya had been working at a frozen yogurt shop for two weeks. One evening she
> was helping another employee named Kathy clean up after the store closed.
>
> Kathy said, "My friend is waiting for me. Let's just rinse these mixers off and put
> them away. No one will know whether we really cleaned them or not. I want to get
> out of here!"
>
> Tanya knew a dirty mixer could cause problems. People who ate yogurt from a
> dirty mixer might get sick. Tanya had to decide what to do.

1. Choice A: Tanya could put the mixers away dirty and say nothing.

   Possible results: _____

   _____

2. Choice B: Tanya could put the mixers away dirty. In the morning, she could
   tell the store manager what Kathy did.

   Possible results: _____

   _____

3. Choice C: Tanya could stay and clean the mixers herself.

   Possible results: _____

   _____

4. Choice D: Tanya could try to convince Kathy to stay and help clean the mixers.

   Possible results: _____

   _____

5. Now explain which choice you think will have the best results, and why.

   _____

   _____

Pacemaker® Skills for Independent Living   Copyright © by Pearson Education, Inc., publishing as Globe Fearon. All rights reserved.

Name_____   Date_____

Think of someone who you think has made a wise decision recently.
This might be someone you know or someone you have read or heard
about. It might be a relative, a neighbor, or a friend. You could even
look in a newspaper or magazine for ideas.

Once you have thought about this person's decision, answer the
questions below. Do not write anything that might embarrass someone.

1. What decision did this person make?

_____

_____

_____

2. What were some other choices the person could have made?

_____

_____

_____

3. Many people think these qualities are important: honesty, responsibility, courage,
concern for others, respect for others, staying healthy, and good citizenship. Which
of these qualities do you think guided this person's decision? Why?

_____

_____

_____

4. Why do you think this person's decision was wise?

_____

_____

_____

Pacemaker® Skills for Independent Living   Copyright © by Pearson Education, Inc., publishing as Globe Fearon. All rights reserved.

Name_____ Date_____

Read each situation below. Write an excuse someone might use to avoid taking responsibility for the action. Then write a responsible action for each one. The first one is done for you.

1. Shelly lost Kara's sweater. Now Kara is angry.

    a. An excuse Shelly might give:

    Shelly tells Kara, "You never should have loaned me that sweater if it was so important to you."

    b. A responsible action Shelly could take:

    Shelly buys Kara a new sweater.

2. Kamal did not make the track team.

    a. An excuse Kamal might give:

    _____

    _____

    b. A responsible action he could take:

    _____

    _____

3. Jeff was supposed to start dinner when he got home from school. He forgot to do it, and his family was angry.

    a. An excuse Jeff might give:

    _____

    _____

    b. A responsible action he might take:

    _____

    _____

Pacemaker® Skills for Independent Living   Copyright © by Pearson Education, Inc., publishing as Globe Fearon. All rights reserved.

Name_____   Date_____

2 ▸ Setting Priorities

Skills 2.1–2.2

Exercise 5
Practice

Read the information about Evan below. Then fill in the chart to help
Evan set his priorities. First fill in his goals based on the information.
Then mark the priority of each item. Use A for a high priority, B for a
medium priority, and C for a low priority. After you have completed the
chart, answer the question that follows.

- Evan likes to play the piano and wants to take lessons so he can play better.

- Evan has a good chance of getting a scholarship at the local community college.
  However, he is having trouble with his grade in social studies. To get the
  scholarship, he must bring his social studies grade up to at least a B.

- A new girl sits next to Evan in homeroom, and he would like to get to know
  her better.

- Evan wants to get a job so he can buy a used car some day.

1.

Goal	Priority

2. Compare your chart with a partner's. Discuss the way that you and your partner
ordered Evan's goals. Were they the same? Why or why not?

_____

_____

_____

Pacemaker® Skills for Independent Living   Copyright © by Pearson Education, Inc., publishing as Globe Fearon.   All rights reserved.

2 ▶ Reaching Goals

Skills 2.2–2.4

Exercise 6

Critical Thinking

Carmen is determined to get a part in the school play. Read the following paragraph and the steps in reaching a goal. Then answer the questions below.

> Carmen has read the whole play several times. She has also chosen the character she would like to play. Every evening, Carmen spends an hour in her room reading her character's lines in the play. She knows that her soft voice might keep her from getting the part, so she is practicing speaking loudly. She has carefully marked the date of the tryouts on her calendar. However, Carmen knows several other people will be trying out for the same part. She is still worried she might not get the part.

STEP 1 Write down the goal.

STEP 2 List steps to reach the goal.

STEP 3 Set up a timeline.

STEP 4 Identify any obstacles.

STEP 5 Identify sources of help.

STEP 6 Check your progress.

1. Which step or steps has Carmen overlooked in trying to reach her goal?

_____

_____

_____

2. What else could Carmen do to increase her chances of reaching her goal?

_____

_____

_____

3. Which step do you think is most important for Carmen to follow? Why do you think so?

_____

_____

_____

Pacemaker® Skills for Independent Living Copyright © by Pearson Education, Inc., publishing as Globe Fearon. All rights reserved.

Name _____   Date _____

 2 ▶ **Managing Time**

Skill 2.5

Read the following sayings about time. Circle the saying that you like best. Then answer the questions below.

- It takes time to save time.

- Every minute starts an hour.

- One of these days is none of these days.

- What may be done at any time will be done at no time.

- You will never "find" time for anything. If you want time, you must make it.

1. What do you think the saying you circled means?

_____

_____

_____

_____

2. Why do you like this saying?

_____

_____

_____

_____

3. How might this saying help people manage their time?

_____

_____

_____

_____

Pacemaker® Skills for Independent Living   Copyright © by Pearson Education, Inc., publishing as Globe Fearon. All rights reserved.

Name_____ Date_____

Skills 2.4–2.6

Think about one way that you might waste time. Then follow the steps below to write an action plan that will help you stop wasting time.

Describe the time waster you will get rid of.

_____

_____

STEP 1 Write down your goal.

_____

_____

STEP 2 List steps to reach the goal.

_____

_____

STEP 3 Set up a timeline.

_____

_____

STEP 4 Identify any obstacles in reaching your goal.

_____

_____

STEP 5 Identify sources of help.

_____

_____

STEP 6 Explain how you will check your progress.

_____

_____

Pacemaker® Skills for Independent Living   Copyright © by Pearson Education, Inc., publishing as Globe Fearon. All rights reserved.

Identifying Friends **Exercise 9**

Skills 3.1–3.4 *Critical Thinking*

Read the situation below. Think about whether Stephan is a good friend for Alonzo and Margo. Then answer the questions.

Stephan, Margo, and Alonzo were talking in the hallway one afternoon.

"Alonzo, you are usually a lot more fun," Stephan said. "If you were really my friend, you would come to my party tonight."

Alonzo shrugged his shoulders. "I don't enjoy parties like that, so I'm not going."

"Well, I'm counting on you to show up, Alonzo. You, too, Margo." With that, Stephan walked away.

"Why don't you like Stephan's parties, Alonzo?" Margo asked.

"Well, for one thing, Stephan told me his parents aren't going to be home. I bet they don't even know he's having a party," Alonzo said. "The last time Stephan had a party, his neighbors called the police. I don't want to be there when that happens."

"I've never been to one of Stephan's parties," Margo said, "but I think I should go. I'll tell you all about it on Monday."

1. Is Stephan a good friend for Alonzo? Why or why not?

_____

_____

_____

2. Is Stephan a good friend for Margo? Why or why not?

_____

_____

_____

3. Are Alonzo and Margo good friends for Stephan? Why or why not?

_____

_____

_____

Pacemaker® Skills for Independent Living   Copyright © by Pearson Education, Inc., publishing as Globe Fearon. All rights reserved.

3 ▶ Identifying Peer Pressure

Exercise 10

Skills 3.2–3.3

Practice

A. Read each situation below. Decide whether it is an example of positive or negative peer pressure. Write *P* for *Positive* or *N* for *Negative* on the line.

_____ **1.** Some of your friends want you to join their club. Before you can be part of the club, they tell you that you need to throw a baseball through your neighbor's window.

_____ **2.** You want to cut class to go to the movies. Your best friend tells you not to cut class.

_____ **3.** You are at a party where underage classmates are drinking beer. Someone says, "Drinking is cool. Don't you want to be cool?"

_____ **4.** You are bike riding with a friend. Even though it is against the law, you do not want to wear a helmet. Your friend insists that you wear your helmet.

_____ **5.** You find $100 on the floor of the library. You want to keep it, but your best friend tells you to hand it in to the librarian so it can be claimed.

_____ **6.** You are in science lab. Your friend tells you to mix chemicals. Your teacher already told the class that mixing chemicals is dangerous.

_____ **7.** Your friend joins the school band. She knows you love to play trumpet. She encourages you to try out for the band.

_____ **8.** You find a pack of cigarettes on the ground. Your best friend takes one out for himself and one out for you. He says, "We'll look more mature if we smoke."

B. Now think of a situation in which you faced positive or negative peer pressure. Write about the situation. Describe how you handled it.

_____

_____

_____

_____

_____

_____

_____

Pacemaker® Skills for Independent Living   Copyright © by Pearson Education, Inc., publishing as Globe Fearon. All rights reserved.

Name_____   Date_____

3 ▶ Saying "No"   **Exercise 11**

Skills 3.4–3.5   *Critical Thinking*

Read the situation below. Then answer the questions.

> RJ, Judi, Maya, and Earl had just finished lunch in the school cafeteria. RJ opened his bookbag so the others could see a pack of cigarettes he had hidden in there. "I need a cigarette. Let's go smoke out behind the gym," he said.
>
> Judi started stuffing her things in her bag. She did not look at RJ as she said, "Not today. Maybe tomorrow."
>
> Maya looked calmly at RJ and shook her head. She said, "I don't smoke."
>
> Earl shoved his chair back and stood up. "Are you kidding, RJ?" he shouted. "Do you want to get me thrown off the football team? You're nuts! I'm out of here."

1. Which friend is RJ likely to keep pressuring? Why?

_____

_____

2. What could this person have said or done differently so RJ would not keep up his pressure?

_____

_____

3. Which friend put too much energy in his or her refusal? What problems could this cause?

_____

_____

4. What should this person have said or done differently?

_____

_____

5. Which friend's refusal do you think was best? What made it the best?

_____

_____

Pacemaker® Skills for Independent Living   Copyright © by Pearson Education, Inc., publishing as Globe Fearon. All rights reserved.

Name_____ Date_____

Read the situation below. Then answer the questions.

> When Anna got to a friend's party, she walked into the kitchen. She did not expect to see a keg of beer there. Some teenagers in the kitchen were holding cups of beer and laughing together. Although Anna did not really like the taste of beer, she poured herself a cup.
>
> Tyrone got to the party a little later. He also walked into the kitchen. He saw the keg of beer and noticed some people drinking it. He looked around until he found some soft drinks in a cooler. He took a can and went into the living room to see who else was there.

1. Anna does not like beer, but she still poured herself some.

   a. What do you think Anna told herself?

   _____

   _____

   _____

   b. Was Anna being honest with herself? Explain your answer.

   _____

   _____

   _____

2. Tyrone saw others drinking, but he ignored the beer.

   a. What do you think Tyrone told himself?

   _____

   _____

   _____

   b. Was Tyrone being honest with himself? Explain your answer.

   _____

   _____

   _____

Pacemaker® Skills for Independent Living   Copyright © by Pearson Education, Inc., publishing as Globe Fearon. All rights reserved.

4 **Checking Listening Skills** **Exercise 13**

Skills 4.1–4.2 *Critical Thinking*

Lee thinks he is a good listener. Read the conversations below and see what you think. Decide whether his words and actions show that he is listening to Bernadette.

> *Bernadette:* "Our oral book reports are due tomorrow, and I'm worried."
>
> *Lee:* "I haven't even picked a book yet!"

1. Is this good listening? Explain your answer.

_____

_____

_____

_____

> *Bernadette:* "I'm worried that I'm going to forget what I wanted to say."
>
> *Lee:* (watching someone come into the room) "You should use note cards. That's what I do."

2. Is this good listening? Explain your answer.

_____

_____

_____

_____

> *Bernadette:* "I always feel like everyone is passing notes while I'm talking."
>
> *Lee:* (nodding) "Does that bother you?"

3. Is this good listening? Explain your answer.

_____

_____

_____

_____

Pacemaker® Skills for Independent Living   Copyright © by Pearson Education, Inc., publishing as Globe Fearon. All rights reserved.

Name_____ Date_____

A. To find out what kind of listener you are, fill in the chart below. First, read each good listening skill. Then place a check in the column that tells how often you use that skill.

Good Listening Skills	Often	Sometimes	Never
I pay attention to the person speaking and do not look around the room.			
I let the person talk and do not interrupt.			
I ask questions about what the person is saying.			
I listen for what the person is feeling.			
I summarize what the person said in my own words.			

B. Now look over your completed chart and set a listening goal.

1. Which good listening skill will you try to use more often? Why?

_____

_____

_____

2. How will you remember to use this skill more often?

_____

_____

_____

3. Why is it important to use this skill?

_____

_____

_____

Pacemaker® Skills for Independent Living Copyright © by Pearson Education, Inc., publishing as Globe Fearon. All rights reserved.

Name_____   Date_____

4 ▶ Understanding Body Language

Skills 4.3–4.4

Exercise 15

Critical Thinking

Look at each photo below and read what the person is saying.

Cara: "What you just said hurt my feelings."

Jon: "No, I'm okay. I'm not upset."

1. Do you think Cara means what she is saying? Explain your answer.

_____

_____

_____

_____

_____

_____

2. Do you think Jon means what he is saying? Explain your answer.

_____

_____

_____

_____

_____

_____

Pacemaker® Skills for Independent Living   Copyright © by Pearson Education, Inc., publishing as Globe Fearon. All rights reserved.

Name_____ Date_____

4 ▶ Putting Skills to Work
Skills 4.1–4.5

Exercise 16

Critical Thinking

Rose needs someone to listen to her. Read what she has to say below.
Explain what you would do and say to be a good listener.

Rose tells you, "I cheated on a science test at school. I know it was wrong."

1. Write what you would do to show you are listening.

_____

_____

_____

_____

_____

2. Write what you would say to show you are listening.

_____

_____

_____

_____

_____

3. Now write something you would not say to Rose. Explain why you would not say it.

_____

_____

_____

_____

_____

Pacemaker® Skills for Independent Living   Copyright © by Pearson Education, Inc., publishing as Globe Fearon. All rights reserved.

5 ▶ Recognizing Other Points of View   Exercise 17

Skills 5.1–5.2   *Practice*

**Read each situation below. Then write each person's possible point of
view about the same situation.**

1. Ingrid thinks that Liam is being bossy. He wants to do their science report on
   crystals, and he will not even listen to her ideas.

   a. Write Liam's possible point of view. _____

   _____

   _____

   b. Write Ingrid's possible point of view. _____

   _____

   _____

2. Ahmad thinks Raina is being disrespectful. She was supposed to meet him at
   the movie theater at 8:00 P.M. It is already 8:15, and she is nowhere in sight.

   a. Write Raina's possible point of view. _____

   _____

   _____

   b. Write Ahmad's possible point of view. _____

   _____

   _____

3. Jordan thinks that anyone who chooses to live in a big city must be crazy.

   a. Write Jordan's possible point of view. _____

   _____

   _____

   b. Write another possible point of view. _____

   _____

   _____

Pacemaker® Skills for Independent Living   Copyright © by Pearson Education, Inc., publishing as Globe Fearon. All rights reserved.

5 ► Using "I Messages"   Exercise 18

Skill 5.3   *Practice*

Read the parts of an "I message." Then read the angry responses
below. For each one, write your own "I message" that explains the
person's feelings.

The parts of an "I message"

I feel... *(describe how you feel, such as angry, embarrassed, or worried)*

when you... *(explain what is bothering you)*

because... *(tell why this bothers you).*

---

1. "I will never, ever let you borrow any of my clothes again! You always lose everything!"

   Your "I message":

   I feel _____

   when you _____

   because _____

   _____

2. "You always laugh when I tell you my feelings. I am never telling you another thing!"

   Your "I message":

   I feel _____

   when you _____

   because _____

   _____

3. "You are a lazy slob! Why don't you ever clean up your own dishes?"

   Your "I message":

   I feel _____

   when you _____

   because _____

   _____

Pacemaker® Skills for Independent Living   Copyright © by Pearson Education, Inc., publishing as Globe Fearon. All rights reserved.

Name_____   Date_____

5 ▶ Recognizing Respect in Others

Exercise 19

Skills 5.4–5.5

Critical Thinking

Chandra, Hannah, and Amy are trying to decide which movie to see. Read their conversation below. Then answer the questions.

"Anything you want to see is okay with me," Chandra told her friends.

"But you kept yawning in that action movie we saw last week," Hannah pointed out. "You don't want to see another action movie, do you?"

Chandra shrugged her shoulders. "I don't care."

"Well, I know what I want to see." Amy pointed to an ad in the newspaper. "This is the best movie out now. It has my favorite actors and lots of action." She checked her watch. "It starts in half an hour, so let's get moving. I don't want to miss any of it."

---

1. Does Hannah respect Chandra? How can you tell?

_____

_____

_____

2. Does Amy respect Chandra? How can you tell?

_____

_____

_____

3. Does Chandra respect herself? How can you tell?

_____

_____

_____

4. Who does Amy respect? How can you tell? How could she be more respectful?

_____

_____

_____

Pacemaker® Skills for Independent Living   Copyright © by Pearson Education, Inc., publishing as Globe Fearon. All rights reserved.

5 ▸ Dealing With Anger

Skills 5.5–5.6

Exercise 20

Critical Thinking

Ira and Ruben are arguing in the locker room. Their team just lost an important basketball game. Read their conversation below. Then answer the questions.

> "Why didn't you pass the ball to me?" Ira shouts at Ruben. "I was right under the basket. But you had to take the shot yourself and miss! You cost us that game!"
>
> "I thought I could make three points from where I was!" Ruben shouts back. "Anyway, you missed two foul shots in the third quarter, Ira. If you were a better shot, we would have won that game!"

1. Ruben and Ira are both angry. What are two things that could be making them angry?

_____

_____

_____

_____

_____

2. What are some ways that Ira and Ruben can calm their angry feelings?

_____

_____

_____

_____

3. What calm thoughts could they have shared to help each other feel better about losing the game?

_____

_____

_____

_____

_____

Pacemaker® Skills for Independent Living   Copyright © by Pearson Education, Inc., publishing as Globe Fearon. All rights reserved.

5 ▶ Settling Conflicts   Exercise 21

Skill 5.7   *Critical Thinking*

Read the situation below. Then answer the questions.

> Maria and Keith both have to do a report on ants for biology class. Their reports are due on Monday. Maria has already been to the school library and taken out the only books on ants. Keith could not find any other books for his report but found several Web sites and CD-ROM articles.
>
> Keith says, "Maria, I'd like to use those books, too. Maybe we could get together this weekend. Then we could both use them."
>
> Maria shakes her head. "That won't work. My family is going to my grandmother's for the weekend, and I'm taking the books with me. Sorry."

1. Is this conflict settled? Why or why not?

_____

_____

_____

_____

2. How did Keith try to settle the conflict?

_____

_____

_____

_____

3. What else might Maria and Keith do to settle their conflict?

_____

_____

_____

_____

_____

Pacemaker® Skills for Independent Living   Copyright © by Pearson Education, Inc., publishing as Globe Fearon. All rights reserved.

Name_____   Date_____

During a person's teenage years, it can be difficult to handle all the
changes that occur. Fill in the chart below with changes and responses.
In the response box, write what a person might say, feel, or do because
of the change. The first one is done for you.

Type of Change	Response to the Change
Physical Changes 1. *Growing taller* 2.	*Accept your height. It might still be changing. Millions of people are the same height as you.*
Emotional Changes 3. 4.	
Social Changes 5. 6.	
Mental Changes 7. 8.	

Pacemaker® Skills for Independent Living   Copyright © by Pearson Education, Inc., publishing as Globe Fearon. All rights reserved.

6 ▶ Conducting an Interview

Skills 6.2–6.3

Exercise 23

Find out how someone you know handled change during the teenage years. Interview one person who is at least 20 years old. This person should be someone you are comfortable with. Try a family member, neighbor, teacher, coach, or friend.

A. Ask the questions below, plus any others that you think are important. Avoid any questions that might embarrass the person you are interviewing.

    1. What kinds of changes happened to you during your teenage years?

_____

_____

    2. How did you feel about these changes?

_____

_____

    3. What helped you deal with these changes?

_____

_____

    4. What advice do you have for young people who are experiencing these changes now?

_____

_____

B. After everyone has completed an interview, discuss what you learned with a group. Then list three things the group found out about teenage changes. Share these findings with the rest of the class.

Here is what my group learned from our interviews.

_____

_____

_____

_____

Pacemaker® Skills for Independent Living   Copyright © by Pearson Education, Inc., publishing as Globe Fearon. All rights reserved.

6 ▸ Writing a Letter of Advice   Exercise 24
Skills 6.4–6.5   *Practice*

**Families face many changes over the years. They might experience
changes in the people who belong to the family or the people who live
at home. Families might also have to deal with a member's illness, a
change in income, or a move to another city or state. To think about
family changes, follow the steps below.**

1. Create a fictional family that includes a teenager. Describe the family members. Give
   their ages. Include all the information you think is important about the family. For
   example, decide where they live and work.

   _____

   _____

   _____

   _____

2. Think of a way this family might change. Describe the change.

   _____

   _____

   _____

   _____

3. Write a letter to the teenager in the family. Suggest ways to deal with this kind of
   family change.

   Dear _____,

   _____

   _____

   _____

   _____

   _____

                                        _____

                                        _____

Pacemaker® Skills for Independent Living   Copyright © by Pearson Education, Inc., publishing as Globe Fearon. All rights reserved.

Name_____   Date_____

 6 ▷ **Creating a Poster**   **Exercise 25**

Skills 6.2–6.4, 6.7   *Practice*

Think of a common cause of stress that many young people have. Then design a poster that explains two or more ways for dealing with stress. Make your poster clear, helpful, and colorful. Suggest ways to deal with stress that are practical. Use the space below to draw the poster. Make sure your poster does not show anything that might embarrass people.

Pacemaker® Skills for Independent Living   Copyright © by Pearson Education, Inc., publishing as Globe Fearon. All rights reserved.

Name_____ Date_____

A. Look through a newspaper to find four articles that show how your community is changing. Copy or paste the headlines in the box below.

```



```

B. Read over your collection of articles. Then fill in the chart below.

Type of Change in the Community	Ways the Change Affects Your Family	Is the Change Positive or Negative?
1.		
2.		
3.		
4.		

Pacemaker® Skills for Independent Living   Copyright © by Pearson Education, Inc., publishing as Globe Fearon. All rights reserved.

7 ▶ Planning Healthful Meals

Skills 7.1–7.4

Exercise 27

Critical Thinking

**You are planning your own meals for a day. Answer the questions below.
Then write your plan for a healthy breakfast, lunch, dinner, and snacks.**

1. Which is better for your breakfast, a chocolate covered donut or a bowl of cereal with a piece of fruit? Why?

   _____

   _____

2. For lunch, you have a choice of meat bologna or oven roasted turkey breast, on either whole wheat bread or white bread. The drink choices are skim milk, apple juice, tomato juice, or soda. What would you choose for the most healthful lunch? Why?

   _____

   _____

3. You find a few snack foods in the kitchen closet. The Nutrition Facts label on the animal crackers says that each serving has 250 calories, with 80 calories from fat. The label on the graham crackers says that each serving has 130 calories, with 30 calories from fat. Which snack is more healthful?

   _____

   _____

4. Your mother has asked you to eat the vegetables she has in the refrigerator. What is the most healthful way to cook them?

   _____

   _____

5. Healthy Food Plan:

   Breakfast _____

   Lunch _____

   Dinner _____

   Snack _____

Pacemaker® Skills for Independent Living   Copyright © by Pearson Education, Inc., publishing as Globe Fearon. All rights reserved.

Name_____ Date_____

 7 **Evaluating Fitness Programs** **Exercise 28**

Skill 7.5 *Critical Thinking*

Josh thinks he gets enough exercise to stay fit. Read the paragraphs below. Then answer the questions.

> Josh studies several evenings a week in his bedroom. During the evening, he reads and works on his computer.
>
> At least once every hour, Josh exercises by running downstairs to the kitchen. He usually goes down to get a snack, such as fruit or a bagel. Other times, he runs downstairs to phone his friends and find out what they are doing. Then he runs back upstairs to his room.

1. Does running up and down one set of stairs make your heart work harder? Why or why not?

_____

_____

_____

2. Is running up and down one set of stairs once an hour aerobic exercise? Why or why not?

_____

_____

_____

3. If this is Josh's total exercise program, will he stay fit? Why or why not?

_____

_____

_____

4. What advice can you give Josh about staying fit?

_____

_____

_____

Pacemaker® Skills for Independent Living   Copyright © by Pearson Education, Inc., publishing as Globe Fearon. All rights reserved.

7 ▶ Writing a Letter of Advice

Skills 7.6–7.7

Exercise 29

Practice

Read the situation below about resisting peer pressure. Then plan a letter to your cousin. Decide the points you want to include. Then write the letter.

> You have a cousin who is in the seventh grade and lives in another state. This cousin looks up to you because you are older. Today you got an e-mail from your cousin. His or her best friend is changing and has started to smoke. This friend is pressuring your cousin to start smoking. Your cousin does not know what to do.

1. Points I want to include in the letter are:

_____

_____

_____

_____

2.

Dear Cousin,

_____

_____

_____

_____

_____

_____

_____

_____

_____

Pacemaker® Skills for Independent Living   Copyright © by Pearson Education, Inc., publishing as Globe Fearon. All rights reserved.

Name_____ Date_____

Skill 7.8   *Critical Thinking*

On a separate sheet of paper, list places near your school or in your community where a person walking alone might be in danger. For example, maybe the neighborhood includes empty buildings. Maybe big trees block the light from streetlights. Maybe people who cause trouble tend to gather at a certain store or mall.

Share your ideas with the class. Then discuss these questions. Write your answers on the lines.

1. Did several people list the same places? If so, what does this tell you?

_____

_____

_____

2. What do the places listed have in common?

_____

_____

_____

3. Did only one person list a certain place? Why might that happen?

_____

_____

_____

4. Will today's discussion change where you go in the community or whether you go out alone? If so, how?

_____

_____

5. What might be done to make any dangerous places in your community safer for everyone?

_____

_____

Pacemaker® Skills for Independent Living   Copyright © by Pearson Education, Inc., publishing as Globe Fearon. All rights reserved.

8 ▶ Understanding Types of Doctors

Skills 8.1–8.2

Exercise 31

Critical Thinking

Doctors are listed under various headings in the Yellow Pages of the phone book. To find the right kind of doctor, you need to understand what the headings mean. Read the chart below. Then read each sentence. On the line, write the kind of doctor each person would want to see.

Word Part	Definition	Kind of Doctor
derma- or dermo-	relating to skin	dermatologist
obstetric-	relating to childbirth	obstetrician
ophthalmo-	relating to eyes	ophthalmologist
ortho-	relating to bones	orthopedist
ped- or pedo-	relating to children	pediatrician
pod-	relating to feet	podiatrist
psych-	relating to the mind	psychiatrist

1. Liu has a mysterious rash.

_____

2. Darnell's feet hurt when he walks.

_____

3. In the emergency room at the hospital, Keisha learns that her knee is broken.

_____

4. Marco feels depressed.

_____

5. Maria's baby brother needs his shots.

_____

6. Shannon's older sister is pregnant and needs to be checked.

_____

7. Javier has trouble reading small type.

_____

Pacemaker® Skills for Independent Living   Copyright © by Pearson Education, Inc., publishing as Globe Fearon. All rights reserved.

Name_____ Date_____

8 ▶ Making Decisions About Medicine   **Exercise 32**
Skill 8.3   *Critical Thinking*

Lina thinks she is doing Benjamin a favor. Read the situation below, and see if you agree. Then answer the questions.

> Lina and Benjamin were walking home from school. Benjamin kept walking slower and slower. "I feel terrible," he moaned. "My throat is killing me."
>
> "I had a sore throat just last week," Lina said. "When I went to the doctor, he gave me a prescription for some pills. I have some left. When we get to my house, I'll give them to you. They really helped me a lot. I feel fine now."
>
> "Are you sure I should take them?" Benjamin asked. "I'm already taking some medicine my mom gave me."
>
> "Sure! It says right on the label how many pills to take and how often to take them," Lina told him.

1. Should Benjamin take Lina's pills? Why or why not?

_____

_____

_____

_____

2. Do the directions on the label mean that anyone can take that medicine? Why or why not?

_____

_____

_____

_____

3. What should Benjamin do if he is feeling sick?

_____

_____

_____

_____

Pacemaker® Skills for Independent Living   Copyright © by Pearson Education, Inc., publishing as Globe Fearon. All rights reserved.

Name_____   Date_____

8 ▶ Analyzing Insurance
Skill 8.4

Exercise 33
Critical Thinking

Choosing an insurance plan can be a difficult decision. Read about
Plan A and Plan B in the chart below. Then list some advantages and
disadvantages for each plan. Decide which one you would choose.

	Plan A	Plan B
Costs	$150 per month	$200 per month
Doctors	Chosen by insurance company	Chosen by you
Covered costs for doctor visits and hospital	This plan covers 100% of doctor visits, including physicals. There is no charge for a hospital stay if you go to a hospital selected by the insurance company.	You pay the first $500 per year of any medical expense. Then the insurance company pays 80% of all other costs.
Prescriptions	$10 per prescription	$10 per prescription

1. *Plan A*

   a. Advantages: _____

   _____

   _____

   b. Disadvantages: _____

   _____

   _____

2. *Plan B*

   a. Advantages: _____

   _____

   _____

   b. Disadvantages: _____

   _____

   _____

3. Which plan would you choose? Why? _____

   _____

Pacemaker® Skills for Independent Living   Copyright © by Pearson Education, Inc., publishing as Globe Fearon. All rights reserved.

9 ▶ Rating Risks

Exercise 34

Skills 9.1–9.2

A. Decide which of the risks below teenagers are most likely to face. Then put the risks in order, starting with 1 for the highest risk and 12 for the lowest.

Possible Risks at Home and Away

_____ fire	_____ falls	_____ car accidents
_____ poisoning	_____ cuts	_____ head wounds
_____ electrical shock	_____ falling objects	_____ slipping
_____ bicycle crashes	_____ broken bones	_____ swimming troubles

Share your ratings with the class. Discuss any differences in the way people rated the risks.

B. Answer the questions below.

1. Which two risks did you rate the highest for teenagers? Why?

   _____

   _____

   _____

   _____

   _____

   _____

2. Which two risks did you rate the lowest for teenagers? Why?

   _____

   _____

   _____

   _____

   _____

   _____

Pacemaker® Skills for Independent Living   Copyright © by Pearson Education, Inc., publishing as Globe Fearon. All rights reserved.

Name_____ Date_____

 9 ▶ **Planning for an Emergency**   **Exercise 35**

Skill 9.3   *Practice*

Do you have a plan for emergencies at home? In the boxes below, draw
the rooms in your home. Use both boxes if your home has two floors.
From each room, draw a green arrow to the exit you would use in case
of fire. Then from each room, draw a yellow arrow to an exit you could
use if the first exit is blocked.

Downstairs

Upstairs

Pacemaker® Skills for Independent Living   Copyright © by Pearson Education, Inc., publishing as Globe Fearon. All rights reserved.

Name_____ Date_____

9 ▶ Handling an Emergency

Skill 9.4

Exercise 36

**Handling an emergency in your home can be difficult. However,
dealing with an emergency in someone else's home can be even harder.
Read the situation below. Then answer the questions.**

> Kyle was helping his neighbor, Mrs. Tanaka, clean her small dark basement.
> Mrs. Tanaka was carrying a box up the old wooden stairs when her foot slipped.
> She lost her balance and fell backward into the basement. She hurt her leg and
> could not stand.

1. Kyle knows Mrs. Tanaka needs help. What should he do?

_____

_____

_____

_____

_____

2. What are some things that could have been done to avoid this emergency?

_____

_____

_____

_____

3. How would you handle this emergency?

_____

_____

_____

_____

_____

Pacemaker® Skills for Independent Living   Copyright © by Pearson Education, Inc., publishing as Globe Fearon. All rights reserved.

Name_____ Date_____

Skill 10.1   *Critical Thinking*

A. List three personal qualities that you think would be important for each job below. Some examples of personal qualities are carefulness, friendliness, fairness, and independence. You may think of many other qualities to put on your list.

Job	Personal Qualities Needed
Bank Teller	a. _____ b. _____ c. _____
Emergency Medical Technician	a. _____ b. _____ c. _____
Welder	a. _____ b. _____ c. _____

B. Answer the questions below.

1. How could you find out which qualities are actually needed for a certain job?

_____

_____

2. Why is it important to learn which personal qualities are necessary for a job?

_____

_____

3. What are three personal qualities that you have?

_____

_____

Pacemaker® Skills for Independent Living Copyright © by Pearson Education, Inc., publishing as Globe Fearon. All rights reserved.

10 ▷ Using "Help Wanted" Ads

Skills 10.2–10.3

Complete the exercises below.

1. On the lines below, list the needs and interests you would like a job to fill. Then find two newspaper "Help Wanted" ads that agree with your list. Cut them out and paste them in the box.

   _____

   _____

   [empty box]

2. Now choose one of your ads. Suppose you were going to call and ask about the job. Write three questions you would ask that are not answered in the ad. Your questions might help you decide whether you want the job and whether you are qualified for it.

   a. _____

   _____

   b. _____

   _____

   c. _____

   _____

Pacemaker® Skills for Independent Living   Copyright © by Pearson Education, Inc., publishing as Globe Fearon. All rights reserved.

10 ▶ Matching Jobs and People

Skills 10.2–10.5

Exercise 39

Practice

Look through these "Help Wanted" ads. Then find a job for each person mentioned below. Explain why you chose that job.

Help Wanted   2156

STEVE STEAMER CLEANERS
Carpet cleaning technicians

Training and career oppor. Latest equipment and van. Benefits, ins. Call Steve Steamer, **555-1860**

Expert repair person M/F. Minimum 15 years experience. Excellent wages. Company truck. Call 555-2113

THE BAGEL SHOP
Customer service. No evening hours. The Bagel Shop needs friendly people to help our customers. Flexible hrs/oppor. for advancement.

CALL 555-2989

Salesperson needed for weekends and evenings. Apply in person at Unfinished Wood Prod., 4769 Sawmill Rd.

P/T office help needed for apartment community. Must be well organized and flexible. Call 555-5813

NURSE'S AIDE
Certificate not necessary. Needed for all shifts in assisted-living facility. Call 555-5823

1. Wanda is outgoing. She is taking business courses at the community college during the day.

Wanda should apply for the job of _____

because _____

_____

2. Hank would like to have his own business someday, but he is not sure what it would be. He likes to work with his hands.

Hank should apply for the job of _____

because _____

_____

3. Cindy is taking courses so she can become a licensed practical nurse (LPN). She knows she will have a lot of competition when she is ready to apply for a job as an LPN.

Cindy should apply for the job of _____

because _____

_____

Pacemaker® Skills for Independent Living   Copyright © by Pearson Education, Inc., publishing as Globe Fearon. All rights reserved.

10 ▶ Writing a Letter of Advice

Skills 10.4–10.5

Exercise 40

Practice

Your friend who lives in another state will graduate soon. This friend wants to get a job but does not know which one would be best.

Write a letter to your friend explaining how to identify the right job. Describe at least two ways to find out more about jobs that seem interesting. Explain how to figure out which jobs are available in the community. Encourage your friend to conduct an informational interview.

_____

Dear _____,

_____

_____

_____

_____

_____

_____

_____

_____

_____

_____

_____

_____

_____

_____

_____

Pacemaker® Skills for Independent Living   Copyright © by Pearson Education, Inc., publishing as Globe Fearon. All rights reserved.

11 ▶ Writing a Résumé and Cover Letter — Exercise 41

Skills 11.1–11.3

To write your own résumé, fill in the information below. Then write or type your résumé and a cover letter on another sheet of paper. Remember, your name, address, and phone number go at the top of the page.

Job Objective (the kind of job you want) _____

Education (the names of the schools you have attended and the year you graduated or will graduate from each one)

_____

(any special courses or training you have had) _____

Experience

_____ (company name) _____

(the date you started
the job you have now) (your job title) _____

(your job responsibilities; include details that show you are doing a good job and are a trusted employee)

_____

_____

_____ (company name) _____

(the dates you started
and ended an earlier job) (your job title) _____

(your job responsibilities) _____

_____

_____

Skills (skills, interests, honors, or awards that relate to this job)

_____

_____

References (people who know you and can recommend you)

_____

_____

Pacemaker® Skills for Independent Living   Copyright © by Pearson Education, Inc., publishing as Globe Fearon. All rights reserved.

Name_____ Date_____

11 ▸ Describing Yourself

Skill 11.4

Think of a job you might like to apply for. Then fill in the job application below.

APPLICATION FOR EMPLOYMENT

Date: _____

Personal Information

Name: _____ Social Security Number: _____

Address: _____
         Street and Number   *City*   *State*   *Zip Code*

Number of years at this address: _____ Phone: _____

Are you 18 years of age or older? ☐ Yes ☐ No

Job you are applying for: _____ Hourly pay expected: _____

Date when you can start working: _____

Education

	Name and address	Number of years there	Graduated: yes/no	Course or major
High school				
College				
Graduate school				
Trade school				

Military Service

Served in U.S. Armed Forces? ☐ Yes ☐ No Branch of Service: _____

Work Experience

Company name and address	Dates of employment	Supervisor's name	Job title	Salary	Reason for leaving

References

Name and occupation   Address   Phone   Years acquainted

_____

_____

_____

I certify that the information I have provided is true. I understand that if you find any deliberate errors, I will not be considered for employment.

_____   _____
Signature   *Date*

Pacemaker® Skills for Independent Living Copyright © by Pearson Education, Inc., publishing as Globe Fearon. All rights reserved.

Name _____ Date _____

11 ▸ Building Interviewing Skills

Skill 11.5

Exercise 43

Ron is interviewing for a job as a salesperson in a clothing store. Read his interview below. Then rewrite the interview in a way that might help *you* get the same job.

Interviewer: Tell me about yourself.

   Ron: Well, I'm 17 and I go to Columbus High. My parents' names are Jeff and Carla, but they are divorced now. I have a younger brother.

Interviewer: I see. Why do you want to work for this store?

   Ron: It doesn't matter where I work. I just want a job.

Interviewer: Our salespeople stock the shelves and racks and keep them neat. How do you feel about that?

   Ron: I'll do it if I have to, but I'd rather just sell stuff.

Interviewer: Well, thank you for coming in, Ron. We'll call you by Friday if we choose you for the job.

Your Interview

Interviewer: Tell me about yourself.

   You: _____

    _____

    _____

Interviewer: Why do you want to work for this store?

   You: _____

    _____

    _____

Interviewer: Our salespeople stock the shelves and racks and keep them neat. How do you feel about that?

   You: _____

    _____

    _____

Interviewer: Well, thank you for coming in. We'll call you by Friday if we choose you for the job.

Pacemaker® Skills for Independent Living   Copyright © by Pearson Education, Inc., publishing as Globe Fearon. All rights reserved.

11 ▶ Choosing Between Jobs

Skill 11.6

Exercise 44

Critical Thinking

Read about Annette and her two job choices. Explain why she might and might not like each job. Then recommend the job you think she should take.

> Annette will graduate from high school next month. She is shy but gets over it after a while. She is patient and good at taking care of details. Her favorite courses in high school are math and data processing. Annette likes to hike and camp with her friends and family.

Bank Teller: Annette would begin this job by spending a month at four different bank offices. She would help people cash checks and make deposits. Tellers must firmly ask for identification each time someone wants to cash a check. The job pays $10.00 an hour. After her training, Annette would work at an office that is a 10-minute bus ride from her home.

1. Why might Annette like this job? _____

_____

2. Why might she not like this job? _____

_____

Surveyor: This job at an engineering company involves mapping out roads. Annette would work on a team, measuring distances. Then the team would use its measurements to draw maps. The job pays $9.00 an hour and is a 30-minute bus ride from Annette's home.

3. Why might Annette like this job? _____

_____

4. Why might she not like this job? _____

_____

5. Here is the job I recommend for Annette and the reasons I recommend it.

_____

_____

_____

_____

Pacemaker® Skills for Independent Living   Copyright © by Pearson Education, Inc., publishing as Globe Fearon. All rights reserved.

12 ▶ Creating a Handbook

Skill 12.1

Exercise 45

Critical Thinking

Right now, your job is going to school. Like most companies, many schools have handbooks that describe the way things work. If your school has a student handbook, do not look through it until you have finished this activity.

Employee and student handbooks begin with a table of contents. This page lists the topics covered in the handbook. For example, an employee handbook might list the company's departments and what they each do. It probably lists company rules. It might also list job benefits.

Create a table of contents for a student handbook for your school. Think about what students at your school need to know. Then list the topics that should be included in the student handbook. Use another sheet of paper if you need more space. The first entry is done for you.

School Handbook
Table of Contents

1. *Student Dress Code* _____

   a. *Clothes that can be worn by students in school* _____

   b. *Clothes that cannot be worn by students in school* _____

2. _____

   a. _____

   b. _____

3. _____

   a. _____

   b. _____

4. _____

   a. _____

   b. _____

5. _____

   a. _____

   b. _____

Pacemaker® Skills for Independent Living   Copyright © by Pearson Education, Inc., publishing as Globe Fearon. All rights reserved.

12 ▶ Identifying Responsible Behavior

Exercise 46

Skills 12.2, 12.5

Critical Thinking

Being responsible is very important for keeping a job. But it is sometimes difficult to know what actions are responsible. Read each situation below. Then write a responsible answer for it.

1. You work in the locker room of a swimming pool. The pool provides free towels for swimmers. One man thinks there is a one dollar charge for the towel. He speaks a language you do not understand. Your co-worker whispers, "Take his money and keep it. That's what I do." The man keeps handing you his dollar.

   a. What should you do? _____

   _____

   _____

   _____

   b. Why? _____

   _____

   _____

   _____

2. Where you work, employees use a time clock. One morning your co-worker calls you from home. She overslept and wants you to clock her in. It will take her an hour to get to work, but she does not want the boss to know she is not there.

   a. What should you do? _____

   _____

   _____

   _____

   b. Why? _____

   _____

   _____

   _____

Pacemaker® Skills for Independent Living   Copyright © by Pearson Education, Inc., publishing as Globe Fearon. All rights reserved.

12 ▶ Working With Customers

Skill 12.3

Exercise 47

Jack just started his new job at a dry cleaning shop. He helps customers who bring in clothing to be cleaned. Read the conversation below and answer the questions about it.

> *Jack:* What do you want?
>
> *Customer:* I have some shirts to be dry cleaned. There are three.
> No, maybe I have four of them.
>
> *Jack:* Well, which is it?
>
> *Customer:* Four, I guess.
>
> *Jack:* Maybe I'd better count them myself.
>
> *Customer:* Never mind. I'll take them to another dry cleaner.

1. Why do you think the customer decided to go to another dry cleaner?

_____

_____

_____

2. Rewrite the conversation above, showing how you would treat the customer with more respect.

> *You:* _____
>
> _____
>
> *Customer:* I have some shirts to be dry cleaned. There are three.
> No, maybe I have four of them.
>
> *You:* _____
>
> _____
>
> *Customer:* I'd like them with not too much starch and on hangers.
>
> *You:* _____
>
> _____
>
> *Customer:* _____
>
> _____

Pacemaker® Skills for Independent Living   Copyright © by Pearson Education, Inc., publishing as Globe Fearon. All rights reserved.

12 ▶ Conducting an Interview

Skill 12.4

Exercise 48

A. Find out if employees need to learn new skills on their jobs. Interview someone who has had the same job for at least one year. You might interview a family member, a neighbor, or a friend. Ask the person you interview the questions below.

1. What is your job?

_____

_____

2. How long have you had it?

_____

_____

3. What new skills have you learned since you started this job?

_____

_____

4. Have you attended any courses, training sessions, or classes related to this job? If so, what did you learn?

_____

_____

5. How have these new skills and knowledge helped you on your job?

_____

_____

B. After your interview, discuss what you learned with a group of classmates. Then answer the question below.

Does every employee need to learn new skills on the job? Why or why not?

_____

_____

_____

Pacemaker® Skills for Independent Living   Copyright © by Pearson Education, Inc., publishing as Globe Fearon. All rights reserved.

Name_____ Date_____

12 ▶ **Looking at Teamwork**
Skill 12.6

Exercise 49
Critical Thinking

Read the following situations. Then answer the questions.

1. Colleen and Ming-na both work in a snack shop. Colleen likes to cook, so she prepares the salads and sandwiches. Ming-na likes to talk to people, so she takes the customers' orders and keeps the front counter and tables clean.

 Are Colleen and Ming-na working as a team? Why or why not?

 _____

 _____

 _____

2. Marco and James have started a lawn-mowing service. They each paid half of the cost of a lawn mower. They put up flyers and asked customers to call the phone number at Marco's house. Marco says he cannot mow any lawns. He has to stay home so he can answer the phone and schedule the customers. James mows all the lawns. Marco takes half of the money they make and gives the other half to James. Marco uses some of his money to go out with his friends in the evening. James is too tired to go out.

 Are Marco and James working as a team? Why or why not?

 _____

 _____

 _____

3. Brenda and Aaron work at a computer factory. They glue in the computer parts. Several times a day, Aaron finds mistakes in the way Brenda glues in a part. "So what?" Brenda says. "If the computer doesn't work, the customer will just bring it back and get another one." Aaron often tries to fix her mistakes so the computers will work correctly.

 Are Brenda and Aaron working as a team? Why or why not?

 _____

 _____

 _____

Pacemaker® Skills for Independent Living   Copyright © by Pearson Education, Inc., publishing as Globe Fearon. All rights reserved.

13 ▶ Charting a Career Path

Skills 13.1–13.3

Emily wants to own a clothing shop someday. She will be graduating from high school in two years.

Write the steps Emily could take to meet her goal. Include two steps she could complete while she is still taking classes. Then show how she will continue to work toward her goal. Add more steps to the diagram if you need more.

Pacemaker® Skills for Independent Living   Copyright © by Pearson Education, Inc., publishing as Globe Fearon. All rights reserved.

13 ▶ Building Trust at Work

Skill 13.3

Exercise 51

Critical Thinking

Read about Samuel's day at work at a copying service center. List four things he did that might make his supervisor trust him. Then list four actions that might make his supervisor not trust him.

> Samuel got to work on time and went right to his work station. He looked through the copying jobs he was supposed to do that day. Then he arranged them from the easiest to the hardest. He realized that he probably would not finish them all. He decided to let the employee who worked the evening shift do the hardest jobs.
>
> Samuel finished the first two jobs. He put them neatly in labeled envelopes for the customers. Then it was his break time. He went to the employees' workroom and called his girlfriend. He had to take an extra five minutes for his break. He needed the time to explain to his girlfriend why he had not called her the night before.
>
> Then Samuel went back to work. His supervisor brought over a rush order that Samuel took care of right away. Then Samuel decided that he needed an extra break. He went back to the workroom and called his girlfriend again.
>
> By quitting time, Samuel had three jobs left to do. He left them for the employee who worked the evening shift.

1. Samuel might gain his supervisor's trust because he

    a. _____

    b. _____

    c. _____

    d. _____

2. Samuel might lose his supervisor's trust because he

    a. _____

    b. _____

    c. _____

    d. _____

Pacemaker® Skills for Independent Living   Copyright © by Pearson Education, Inc., publishing as Globe Fearon. All rights reserved.

13 ▸ Rating Yourself

Skill 13.4

Exercise 52

A. Fill out your own review for your job as a student. Then answer the question that follows.

Name of School: _____

Student: _____   Date: _____

Year/Grade: _____   Review: ____9th Week____

	Above Average	Average	Needs Improvement
1. Attends class every day on time			
2. Has a positive attitude toward school			
3. Studies at least one hour before major tests			
4. Completes work that is assigned			
5. Asks for help when necessary			
6. Works to the best of his or her abilities			
7. Relates well to other students			
8. Follows school rules			
9. Takes part in school activities			
10. Shows respect for teachers and staff			

B. Which of the numbered statements above might be on a real job review? Write the statements on the lines below.

_____

_____

_____

_____

_____

Pacemaker® Skills for Independent Living   Copyright © by Pearson Education, Inc., publishing as Globe Fearon. All rights reserved.

Name_____ Date_____

You have been working at Creamy's Ice Cream Parlor for four months. Your employer calls you in for a job review. Answer the questions below.

1. What can happen at a job review? List at least three things.

_____

_____

_____

_____

2. Your boss notes you are good with customers, take direction well, and are very aware of cleanliness and safety rules. Is now a good time to ask for a raise? Why or why not?

_____

_____

_____

_____

3. Your boss asks you to describe areas of your work which you think you should improve. Is now a good time to make excuses for being late? Why or why not?

_____

_____

_____

_____

4. There is an opening at the shop for a weekend manager. The person will have to work three out of the four weekends per month. If your career goal is to own your own food shop, should you apply for the job? Why or why not?

_____

_____

_____

_____

Pacemaker® Skills for Independent Living   Copyright © by Pearson Education, Inc., publishing as Globe Fearon. All rights reserved.

Name_____ Date_____

14 ▶ Setting Bank Rules   Exercise 54

Skills 14.1, 14.4   *Critical Thinking*

A. Your group is setting up a new bank. Decide which types of fees, if any, you will charge and what interest, if any, you will pay. Fill in the chart below. Remember, if your fees are too high, you will not have any customers. If your fees are too low, the bank will not make any money and might go out of business. Choose fees and interest that you think would be fair.

Bank rules	If so, how much?
1. Will a customer have to have a minimum deposit to open an account? Yes No	
2. Will you charge a fee to print customer's names and addresses on their checks? Yes No	
3. Will you charge a monthly fee to keep customer's accounts open? Yes No	
4. Will you charge a fee for each check customers write? Yes No	
5. Will you charge a fee if the money in a customer's account drops below a certain level? Yes No	
6. Will you charge customers a fee to use the bank's ATM machines? Yes No	
7. What other fees will you charge?	
8. Will you pay interest on checking accounts? Yes No	

B. Compare your fees and interest with those of other groups. Based on the fees and interest, choose a bank for your group. Discuss why you chose that bank with group members.

Pacemaker® Skills for Independent Living   Copyright © by Pearson Education, Inc., publishing as Globe Fearon. All rights reserved.

Name _____   Date _____

 14 ► **Writing Checks**   **Exercise 55**
Skill 14.2   *Practice*

Read the information below and fill in each check.

1. Susan needs to pay for groceries that she bought at SuperStore. The total is
   $23.69. Fill out this check as Susan would.

   Susan Kellner   55-555/1234   NO. **143**
   3 Home Street   7654321
   Cincinnati, Ohio 45219

                                         DATE _____

   PAY TO THE
   ORDER OF _____ $ [   ]

   _____ DOLLARS

   Sound Sure Bank
   1 Corporate Square
   Cincinnati, Ohio 45201

   MEMO _____   _____

   ⑈08╖123528⑈   08231041‖

2. Susan also needs to write a check to her brother, Ken Kellner. She borrowed
   $45 from Ken and is now paying him back. Fill out this check as Susan would.

   Susan Kellner   55-555/1234   NO. **144**
   3 Home Street   7654321
   Cincinnati, Ohio 45219

                                         DATE _____

   PAY TO THE
   ORDER OF _____ $ [   ]

   _____ DOLLARS

   Sound Sure Bank
   1 Corporate Square
   Cincinnati, Ohio 45201

   MEMO _____   _____

   ⑈08╖123528⑈   08231041‖

Pacemaker® Skills for Independent Living   Copyright © by Pearson Education, Inc., publishing as Globe Fearon. All rights reserved.

14 ▷ Making a Deposit

Skill 14.2

Exercise 56

Practice

Read the information below and answer the questions.

1. Susan wants to make a bank deposit. She is going to deposit her paycheck of $78.90, plus $23.50 in cash that she earned baby-sitting. She is not going to keep any cash. Fill out her deposit slip for her.

Susan Kellner 3 Home Street Cincinnati, Ohio 45219		CASH	CURRENCY	
			COIN	
		LIST CHECKS SINGLY		
DATE _____ *DEPOSITS MAY NOT BE AVAILABLE FOR IMMEDIATE WITHDRAWAL*				55-555/1234 7654321
SIGN HERE FOR CASH RECEIVED (IF REQUIRED)		**TOTAL**		
Sound Sure Bank 1 Corporate Square Cincinnati, Ohio 45201		LESS CASH RECEIVED		BE SURE EACH ITEM IS PROPERLY ENDORSED
		NET DEPOSIT		

⑈08 7⑈23528⑈ 0823⑈04⑈"

CHECKS AND OTHER ITEMS RECEIVED FOR DEPOSIT ARE SUBJECT TO THE PROVISIONS
OF THE UNIFORM COMMERCIAL OR ANY APPLICABLE COLLECTION AGREEMENT

DEPOSIT TICKET — PLEASE PRESS FIRMLY

2. Susan did not baby-sit this week and is just depositing her paycheck of $78.90. She wants to keep $20 in cash from her paycheck. Fill out her deposit slip for her.

Susan Kellner 3 Home Street Cincinnati, Ohio 45219		CASH	CURRENCY	
			COIN	
		LIST CHECKS SINGLY		
DATE _____ *DEPOSITS MAY NOT BE AVAILABLE FOR IMMEDIATE WITHDRAWAL*				55-555/1234 7654321
SIGN HERE FOR CASH RECEIVED (IF REQUIRED)		**TOTAL**		
Sound Sure Bank 1 Corporate Square Cincinnati, Ohio 45201		LESS CASH RECEIVED		BE SURE EACH ITEM IS PROPERLY ENDORSED
		NET DEPOSIT		

⑈08 7⑈23528⑈ 0823⑈04⑈"

CHECKS AND OTHER ITEMS RECEIVED FOR DEPOSIT ARE SUBJECT TO THE PROVISIONS
OF THE UNIFORM COMMERCIAL OR ANY APPLICABLE COLLECTION AGREEMENT

DEPOSIT TICKET — PLEASE PRESS FIRMLY

Pacemaker® Skills for Independent Living   Copyright © by Pearson Education, Inc., publishing as Globe Fearon. All rights reserved.

Name_____   Date_____

 14 ▶ Keeping a Check Register   **Exercise 57**

Skill 14.3   *Practice*

A. Susan knows she must use a check register to keep track of the money
in her checking account. Fill in Susan's check register for her. Record
check 143 for $23.69 made out to SuperStore on 8/30/01, check 144
for $45 made out to her brother Ken Kellner on 9/4/01, and Susan's
bank deposit of $102.40 made on 9/15/01.

		PLEASE BE SURE TO DEDUCT ANY CHECK CHARGES OR SERVICE CHARGES THAT MAY APPLY TO YOUR ACCOUNT				BALANCE	
NUMBER	DATE	DESCRIPTION OF TRANSACTION	(-) PAYMENT	FEE (IF ANY)	(+) DEPOSIT	$ 253	64
142	8/19/01	Wall Phone Company	41 67			41	67
						211	97
	8/22/01	Deposit			78 90	78	90
						290	87

B. Answer these questions.

1. What is Susan's final balance?

_____

2. Before Susan wrote check 142, was her balance higher or lower than $211.97?
Explain your answer.

_____

3. What is Susan's balance on 9/5/01?

_____

4. Some check registers include a column marked "Fee, if any." What kinds of fees
might this refer to?

_____

Pacemaker® Skills for Independent Living   Copyright © by Pearson Education, Inc., publishing as Globe Fearon. All rights reserved.

Writing a Letter of Advice   **Exercise 58**

Skills 14.1, 14.5   *Practice*

You have received the letter below from your cousin Eric, who lives in another state. He is asking for your advice about managing his money. Write back to Eric, offering some sound advice about managing his money.

Dear Cousin,

I can't decide whether to put my money in a checking account or a savings account.

I make about $63.50 a week working part-time during the school year. I share a car with my brother and pay half of the payments and insurance. That comes to about $180 a month. I spend about $15 a week on movies and snacks after school.

What do you think? Should I put my paycheck into a savings account? I know I would get more interest there.

Sincerely,

Eric

Dear Eric,

_____

_____

_____

_____

_____

_____

_____

_____

Pacemaker® Skills for Independent Living   Copyright © by Pearson Education, Inc., publishing as Globe Fearon. All rights reserved.

15 ▶ Analyzing a Paycheck   Exercise 59

Skill 15.1   *Practice*

Here is a check that Eric received for working at Sydney's Deli. Look it over carefully. Then read the statements below. Write *true* or *false* after each statement. Then explain your choice.

		DATE	CHECK NO.
Sydney's Deli 24 Broad Street Knoxville, TN 37915		07/23/01	1248

PAY   One Hundred and Seventy and forty/100 dollars

AMOUNT
$170.40

TO THE
ORDER OF   Eric Connor
4276 Roberts Lane
Knoxville, TN 37912

SECOND CITY BANK
1 Clarkson Drive
Knoxville, TN 37901   AUTHORIZED SIGNATURE   *Sydney Varner*
ACCOUNTANT

⑈081788000⑈ 0823954⑈

1. Eric lives at 24 Broad Street in Knoxville, TN. Explain your choice.

    _____

2. Eric must cash this check by July 23, 2001. Explain your choice.

    _____

3. Sydney Varner signed this check. Explain your choice.

    _____

4. Sydney's Deli keeps its money at Second City Bank. Explain your choice.

    _____

5. Because $170.40 is written on this check twice, the check can be cashed
    for $340.80. Explain your choice.

    _____

6. Eric wrote in the $170.40 amount. Explain your choice.

    _____

7. This is Eric's 1,248th check from Sydney's Deli. Explain your choice.

    _____

Pacemaker® Skills for Independent Living   Copyright © by Pearson Education, Inc., publishing as Globe Fearon. All rights reserved.

15 ▶ Understanding a Paycheck Stub   Exercise 60

Skill 15.2   *Critical Thinking*

Below is Eric's paycheck stub. He earns $6 an hour at Sydney's Deli.
Study his paycheck stub carefully. Then answer the questions.

EMPLOYEE NAME	EMPLOYEE ID				**Sydney's Deli**	
Conner, Eric	234-98-1009				24 Broad Street	
ISSUE DATE	PAY PERIOD ENDING				Knoxville, TN 37915	
07/23/01	07/20/01					
EARNINGS DESCRIPTION	HOURS	CURRENT	YTD	DEDUCTIONS DESCRIPTION	CURRENT	YTD
Weekly Pay	40	240.00	2160.00	FIT	18.00	162.00
				FICA	36.00	324.00
				State Tax	12.00	108.00
				City Tax	3.60	32.40
				NET PAY	170.40	

STATEMENT OF EARNINGS AND DEDUCTIONS • DETACH AND RETAIN FOR YOUR RECORDS

1. How many different kinds of taxes were taken out of Eric's paycheck?

_____

2. Find 2160.00 under the heading YTD. What is this amount?

_____

3. How much state tax has been deducted from Eric's pay so far this year?

_____

4. If Eric had worked 20 hours instead of 40 hours, what would the number
under the Current heading be?

_____

5. After the deductions are subtracted, is Eric's net pay of $170.40 correct?
How do you know?

_____

Pacemaker® Skills for Independent Living   Copyright © by Pearson Education, Inc., publishing as Globe Fearon. All rights reserved.

15 ▶ Writing a Letter of Advice

Skill 15.3

Exercise 61

Critical Thinking

You write an advice column for a teen magazine. It is called "Advice From Andy." A reader wrote the letter below to you. He wants your advice. Write back to Chris. Where might Chris go to get his check cashed? What might he do to help this situation before he gets his next check?

Dear Andy,

   I am really angry. No one respects teenagers in my town. This afternoon I got my first paycheck from the grocery store where I work. I took it straight to the nearest bank. Do you know what? The teller wouldn't cash it! What can I do to get my check cashed?

                        Your friend,

                        Chris

Dear Chris,

_____

_____

_____

_____

_____

_____

_____

_____

_____

_____

_____

_____

Pacemaker® Skills for Independent Living   Copyright © by Pearson Education, Inc., publishing as Globe Fearon. All rights reserved.

15 ▶ Sorting Out Expenses

Skills 15.4

Exercise 62

Practice

**Help Tony set up his budget. Read below to see how much he earns and
how much he spends. List his income and expenses in the chart. Then
answer the questions that follow.**

"I just got a new job. I also just got a new car. My aunt made the down payment
on the car, but I have to make the monthly payments. They are $125 a month.
Then there is my car insurance. I can't avoid that, no matter how much I would like
to. The insurance payment is due every six months and is about $500.

"Even just having fun costs money. My girlfriend loves to go to the movies. One
week she pays. The next week I do. We usually get ice cream afterwards. It costs me
at least $25 when it is my turn to pay.

"I forgot about gas for my car. So far, that is about $20 a week. But I figure I can
keep it down to $15 if I try.

"I work about 15 hours a week after school. I make $5.50 an hour clearing tables
at a restaurant. But my paycheck is not $82.50. It is only about $65 after taxes.

"So what do you think? Will I have enough money each month?"

1.

Tony's Monthly Income	Tony's Monthly Expenses

2. Figure out whether Tony's income will cover his expenses. Tell him what
you discovered.

_____

_____

_____

3. Give Tony some advice about balancing his budget.

_____

_____

_____

Pacemaker® Skills for Independent Living   Copyright © by Pearson Education, Inc., publishing as Globe Fearon. All rights reserved.

Name_____   Date_____

15 ▸ Calculating Income

Skills 15.4–15.6

Exercise 63

Practice

Marney has just gotten a new part-time job. She will work 20 hours per week and her pay will be $6.00 per hour. Marney asked her boss what her net pay would be, and he gave her the following information.

Each week, the following deductions will be taken out of Marney's paycheck.

Federal tax	15% of gross pay
State tax	5% of gross pay
Social Security tax	7.5% of gross pay
City tax	1.5% of gross pay

Answer the following questions about Marney's income.

1. How much money will be deducted each week for each tax?

   Federal tax _____

   State tax _____

   Social Security tax _____

   City tax _____

2. What will Marney's net pay be each week? _____

3. Marney needs $55.00 each week to cover her expenses. She would like to save enough money to buy a new dress for a party. The dress costs $75, and the party is 15 weeks away. Will Marney be able to save enough to buy the dress?

   _____

   _____

   _____

4. Marney's friend tells her about another job. It pays $7.00 per hour. The same percentages would be deducted from her check each week for taxes. She could work 20 hours per week. Should Marney take the job? Why or why not?

   _____

   _____

   _____

Pacemaker® Skills for Independent Living   Copyright © by Pearson Education, Inc., publishing as Globe Fea·on. All rights reserved.

16 ▸ Shopping Carefully

Skills 16.1–16.4

Exercise 64

A. Suppose you had $100 to spend on clothes. How much could you get for that $100? Use store catalogs, store flyers, or newspaper ads to find clothing that you like. If possible, cut out pictures of the items you chose, plus their prices. Paste or describe them in the box below. Make sure the total cost of the clothing is no more than $100.

Here is how much I could buy for $100.

```



```

B. Answer the following questions based on what you found.

1. Should you always buy the least expensive clothing you can find? Why or why not?

_____

_____

_____

2. Why might you buy one shirt that costs more than another shirt?

_____

_____

_____

3. What are some good reasons *not* to buy the most expensive brand of something, such as jeans?

_____

_____

_____

Pacemaker® Skills for Independent Living   Copyright © by Pearson Education, Inc., publishing as Globe Fearon. All rights reserved.

16 ▶ Comparing Messages   Exercise 65

Skill 16.3   *Critical Thinking*

**Read the six advertising messages below. Then look through magazines
and newspapers for ads that use these messages. Choose two different
products that are being advertised with each message. Answer the
questions.**

1. *Everybody else has one.* Does an ad using this message make you want to buy
these products? Why or why not?

_____

_____

2. *Famous people use this product.* Does an ad using this message make you want
to buy these products? Why or why not?

_____

_____

3. *This product will make you look more attractive.* Does an ad using this message
make you want to buy these products? Why or why not?

_____

_____

4. *Use this product and you will have more fun.* Does an ad using this message
make you want to buy these products? Why or why not?

_____

_____

5. *We are your friends. You can trust us.* Does an ad using this message make
you want to buy these products? Why or why not?

_____

_____

6. *Use this product and you will be in better health.* Does an ad using this message
make you want to buy these products? Why or why not?

_____

_____

Pacemaker® Skills for Independent Living   Copyright © by Pearson Education, Inc., publishing as Globe Fearon. All rights reserved.

16 ▶ Designing an Ad

Skill 16.3

Exercise 66

Critical Thinking

Ads can make almost anything look good. They can sometimes make you want something you normally would not like. The more you know about advertising messages, the better prepared you will be to understand them.

1. Look around the classroom or your home, and find something that you do not like.

2. Design an ad to sell that product, in whatever condition it is in. In your ad, turn any weakness of your product into a selling point. For example, you might be trying to sell a pencil that has been chewed. Your ad might say that the tooth marks show the pencil has many uses, including reducing tension.

3. Try out different ads for your product on scrap paper.

4. Write your best ad below.

_____

_____

_____

_____

_____

_____

_____

_____

_____

_____

_____

_____

Pacemaker® Skills for Independent Living   Copyright © by Pearson Education, Inc., publishing as Globe Fearon. All rights reserved.

16 ▶ Writing Tips for Consumers

Skill 16.4

Exercise 67

Practice

Just for fun, list five tips that would help someone spend a lot of money at a supermarket and still *not* get what he or she needed. Do not list good tips, such as "Before you go to the store, make a list of what you need." Instead, write something like this: "When you get to the store, wander around and buy only interesting things."

Tip 1: _____

_____

Tip 2: _____

_____

Tip 3: _____

_____

Tip 4: _____

_____

Tip 5: _____

_____

After writing your funny tips, answer the following questions.

1. If someone followed your tips, what would be the result?

_____

_____

2. Which tips have you followed without realizing it?

_____

_____

3. Why do you think some people might follow your tips without realizing it?

_____

_____

Pacemaker® Skills for Independent Living   Copyright © by Pearson Education, Inc., publishing as Globe Fearon. All rights reserved.

16 ▶ Judging Actions

Exercise 68

Skills 16.5–16.6

Critical Thinking

Tanisha is angry. She may have caused part of the problem herself. Read what happened and answer the questions.

> Tonya's birthday was in three weeks, so her sister Tanisha bought her a pair of jeans. Tonya was excited when she opened her present and saw the jeans. Yet when she tried them on, she did not like the way they looked on her. "Don't worry," Tanisha said. "I'll take them back and get you something else."
>
> Tanisha searched for the sales slip for the jeans, but she could not find it. However, she took the jeans back to the store anyway.
>
> The clerk said the store would take back the jeans, even though Tanisha did not have the sales slip. However, the jeans were now on sale for much less than Tanisha had paid. The store would only refund the sale price. Tanisha said she had bought the jeans three weeks ago, before the sale.
>
> Tanisha had spent all her money on Tonya's present. If she got a refund for the sale price, she could not buy Tonya something else that was as nice. But if she did not return the jeans, she would end up giving Tonya nothing. Tanisha thought about keeping the jeans for herself, but they didn't fit her at all. What a waste!

1. What was one mistake that Tanisha made?

_____

_____

2. What other mistake did Tanisha make?

_____

_____

3. Do you think the clerk was right to offer to refund only the sale price of the jeans? Why or why not?

_____

_____

4. Suppose Tonya had liked the jeans, but they shrank after she washed them. Do you think the store or the manufacturer would have warranted them without a sales slip? Explain your answer.

_____

_____

Pacemaker® Skills for Independent Living   Copyright © by Pearson Education, Inc., publishing as Globe Fearon. All rights reserved.

Name_____   Date_____

Below is part of a telephone bill Jaime received last month. Study it
and then answer the questions.

 CONSUMER SERVICES
                     Billing Summary

Account Number: 613 555-8720
Date: July 1, 2001

Previous Bill	Payments	Adjustments	Past Due Amount	Current Charges	Total Amount Due
71.77	0.00	0.00	71.77	51.37	123.14

Summary of Current Charges

Ameritech

Monthly Services	25.45
Local Calls	.75
Local and State Additional Charges	.12
Federal Taxes	.79

Total Ameritech Current Charges	27.11

ABC Long Distance Company

Long Distance Charges	24.26

Total Current Charges	**$51.37**

1. How much of last month's phone bill did Jaime pay?

   _____

2. Why is the Total Amount Due higher than the Current Charges?

   _____

3. Jaime still cannot afford to pay his phone bill. He decides he will not pay it
   this month. He also decides that he will not make any more long distance
   phone calls. How much is his phone bill likely to be next month, even if
   the phone company does not add an interest charge or late fee?

   _____

4. What does Jaime risk if he does not pay his phone bill?

   _____

Pacemaker® Skills for Independent Living   Copyright © by Pearson Education, Inc., publishing as Globe Fearon. All rights reserved.

17 ► Analyzing Credit Card Bills

Skills 17.2–17.3

Exercise 70

This is a credit card bill that Amanda received from Rossman's Department Store. Study the bill and use it to answer the questions.

Rossman's Department Store **518 Galena Avenue** **Albany, WI 53502**	**Closing Date:** September 30, 2001 **Payment Due:** October 15, 2001		Page 1

Account Summary	Account Number	6011 2002 5641
	Credit Limit	$ 400.00
	Credit Available	$ 75.60
	Minimum Payment	$ 35.00

Previous Balance	$ 240.62
Payments and Credits	30.00
New Purchases	109.85
FINANCE CHARGES	3.93
New Balance	$ 324.40

Transactions	**Payments and Credits**		
	Sept. 10	Payment – Thank You	$30.00
	Purchases		
	Sept. 18, 2001	Ladies Sportswear	$99.32
	Sept. 18, 2001	Cosmetics	10.53

- -

Please detach and return with your payment.

Account Number: 6011 2002 5641   **Minimum Payment:** $35.00   New Balance: $324.00

Amanda Ruez
850 Pine Street
Albany, WI 53502

Payment
Enclosed $ _____

1. What is Amanda's minimum payment? When is it due?

   _____

2. Did Amanda buy anything with her credit card at Rossman's in the past month? How can you tell?

   _____

3. Which part of the bill needs to be included with Amanda's payment? How do you know?

   _____

Pacemaker® Skills for Independent Living   Copyright © by Pearson Education, Inc., publishing as Globe Fearon. All rights reserved.

Comparing Credit Cards   **Exercise 71**

Skills 17.3–17.4   *Critical Thinking*

A. Fill out the chart below to compare credit cards. You might gather this information by talking to people who have the credit cards or by calling banks or stores that offer credit cards. If you wish, add another type of credit card. Figure out which credit card company has the best offer.

Type of Business Offering Card	Annual Fee		Interest Rate	Place Where This Card Is Accepted
	Yes (How Much?)	No		
1. _____ Bank #1				
2. _____ Bank #2				
3. _____ Clothing store #1				
4. _____ Clothing store #2				
5. _____ Electronics store				
6. _____ Music store				
7. _____ Gas station				

B. Answer the questions below, using the information you gathered.

1. Which card, if any, would you recommend for a young person? Explain your choice.

_____

_____

2. Get an application for the card you chose and complete it. List the type of information it asks for below.

_____

_____

Pacemaker® Skills for Independent Living   Copyright © by Pearson Education, Inc., publishing as Globe Fearon. All rights reserved.

Name_____ Date_____

Being a responsible consumer is not always easy. Companies often call
or write to people, trying to get them to apply for a credit card. Some
companies send credit cards to people who have not even applied for them.

Read the situations below and answer the questions.

1. Alex has credit cards from three local stores. Once she forgot to pay a bill,
and another time her payment was received after the due date. If she applies
for a car loan, do you think she will get it? Why or why not?

_____

_____

_____

2. Sadeq has a gas station credit card. His brother asked to borrow it and
promised to pay the bill, but he did not. Now Sadeq has to pay finance
charges and a late fee. What could he have done differently?

_____

_____

_____

3. Zander got a credit card at the music store. Each month he makes a purchase
or two and then pays the bill as soon as it comes in the mail. If he keeps this
up, do you think Zander will have a good credit report or a bad one? Explain
your answer.

_____

_____

_____

4. Ivy already has four credit cards from four stores. She sometimes has trouble paying
all of her bills. When she buys a sweater at a new department store downtown, the
clerk tells her she can get 10% off of her purchase if she signs up for the store's credit
card. Should she sign up for the credit card? Explain your answer.

_____

_____

_____

Pacemaker® Skills for Independent Living   Copyright © by Pearson Education, Inc., publishing as Globe Fearon. All rights reserved.

18 ▸ Creating an Ad

Skill 18.1

Exercise 73

A. Answer the question below. Then, on another sheet of paper, make a poster to encourage people to take the bus, train, or subway. As you plan your poster, use one of the reasons from your list below. Also, think about the ad messages you have learned about earlier. You might be able to use one of them in your poster. Share your poster with the class.

What are three reasons people should take a bus, train, or subway instead of driving?

1. _____

2. _____

3. _____

B. Answer the questions below with the class.

1. How did listing the reasons for taking a bus, train, or subway help you create an effective poster?

   _____

   _____

   _____

2. Look at the class's posters. Which reasons to take the bus, train, or subway were used most often? Why do you think this is so?

   _____

   _____

   _____

3. What might your community do to encourage more people to use public transportation?

   _____

   _____

   _____

Pacemaker® Skills for Independent Living   Copyright © by Pearson Education, Inc., publishing as Globe Fearon. All rights reserved.

18 ▶ Reading a Bus Schedule

Skill 18.2

Exercise 74

Practice

Before you take a bus, you have to be able to read a bus schedule.
Study the schedule shown below. Then answer the questions.

	Stops on Monday–Friday: Going North			
Bus	**City Center Terminal**	**Broad and High St.**	**Cleveland and Innis St.**	**Cleveland and 161 St.**
A	6:20 A.M.	6:23 A.M.	6:43 A.M.	6:52 A.M.
B	7:04 A.M.	7:07 A.M.	7:28 A.M.	7:37 A.M.
C	7:23 A.M.	7:26 A.M.		
D	7:34 A.M.	7:38 A.M.		
E	7:52 A.M.	7:56 A.M.		
F	8:14 A.M.	8:18 A.M.		
G	8:59 A.M.	9:03 A.M.		
A	3:41 P.M.	3:45 P.M.	4:05 P.M.	4:15 P.M.
B	4:37 P.M.	4:41 P.M.	5:05 P.M.	5:13 P.M.
C	4:49 P.M.	4:55 P.M.	5:17 P.M.	5:29 P.M.
D	5:13 P.M.	5:19 P.M.	5:43 P.M.	5:52 P.M.
E	5:37 P.M.	5:41 P.M.	6:03 P.M.	6:12 P.M.
F	6:13 P.M.	6:17 P.M.	6:38 P.M.	6:47 P.M.

1. What is the latest time you can leave City Center in the morning and get to Broad and High St. by 9:15 A.M.?

   _____

2. If you took the 7:07 A.M. bus at Broad and High St. and you are traveling north to your job at Cleveland and 161 St., would a later morning bus also bring you to work? Why or why not?

   _____

3. If you were at the corner of Cleveland and Innis St. at 5:13 P.M., how long would you have to wait for a bus going north?

   _____

4. What is the latest time in the evening that you could catch a bus going north from the City Center Terminal?

   _____

Pacemaker® Skills for Independent Living   Copyright © by Pearson Education, Inc., publishing as Globe Fearon. All rights reserved.

18 ▶ **Understanding Signs**

Skill 18.3

Could you pass the written driver's license test? The questions below are like the ones on the test. Circle the letter that tells what each sign means.

1.

    a. A sharp turn to the right is ahead.

    b. A sharp turn to the left is ahead.

    c. A crossroad is ahead.

2.

    a. You must ride a bicycle here.

    b. Watch out for people riding bicycles here.

    c. Riding a bicycle is good exercise.

3.

    a. Stop here and check to see if any cars are coming.

    b. Go slowly here.

    c. Other cars will stop for you, so you can keep going.

4.

    a. Do not drive here.

    b. A crossroad is ahead.

    c. A railroad crossing is ahead.

Pacemaker® Skills for Independent Living   Copyright © by Pearson Education, Inc., publishing as Globe Fearon. All rights reserved.

Name_____ Date_____

A. Read the information in the chart below. Then match each type of vehicle with the driver that would most likely use it. Write the correct letter on the line.

Type of Vehicle	Description of Vehicle
a. Small Car	Very good gas mileage; great for commuting; not a lot of extra room for passsengers and storage
b. Mid-Size Car	Good for carpooling and traveling with a small group; good gas mileage
c. Truck	Ideal for someone in the service industry; good for transporting large, heavy items
d. Van	Great passenger vehicle; a lot of room for storage; average gas mileage
e. Sports Utility Vehicle	Good car for people who love to drive and want adventure; poor gas mileage

_____ **1.** Marla has a part-time job and goes to school full-time. She needs a car that gets good gas mileage and is not expensive.

_____ **2.** Joey helps his dad with the family carpet-cleaning business. He is looking for a vehicle to use when he helps his dad.

_____ **3.** Mei comes from a large family. Her parents need a new vehicle to take the family on their monthly visits to relatives in another state.

_____ **4.** Hakeem loves the outdoors. Most of his free time is spent camping, fishing, or hiking. He needs a vehicle to help him get to remote nature sites.

_____ **5.** Justin carpools to work. He needs a new vehicle that can hold at least three other people.

B. Now list the ways that you would use a car. Then choose the car from the chart that would best meet your needs. Explain why you chose that car.

_____

_____

_____

Pacemaker® Skills for Independent Living   Copyright © by Pearson Education, Inc., publishing as Globe Fearon. All rights reserved.

18 ▸ Recognizing Responsible Behavior Exercise 77

Skill 18.5 *Critical Thinking*

Read each situation below. Then decide what you think a responsible driver might do.

1. Jamal is driving to school. He is worried about being late. He needs to make a left turn onto Oak Street. He has to turn across the oncoming traffic lane. A car is coming toward him, so he waits for it to pass. Then he sees another car coming toward him. This car is about half a block away. What would a responsible driver do in Jamal's situation? Remember, he might be late for school unless he hurries.

_____

_____

_____

_____

2. Andrea is driving home. It will take her 15 more minutes to get there. She is really tired, and her eyes keep closing. What would a responsible driver do in Andrea's situation?

_____

_____

_____

_____

3. Mike's old car needs new brakes. Lately, he has had to push on the brake pedal very hard to get the car to stop. However, his friends are going to a concert this weekend. If Mike fixes his car, he will not be able to buy a ticket for the concert. What would a responsible driver do in Mike's situation?

_____

_____

_____

_____

Pacemaker® Skills for Independent Living   Copyright © by Pearson Education, Inc., publishing as Globe Fearon. All rights reserved.

19 ▶ Deciding on Housing

Skill 19.1

Exercise 78

A. When people choose a place to live, they have certain needs and wants. These needs and wants often change as they grow older.

Suppose that you are looking for a new place to live. Read the list of Possible Things to Consider in choosing housing. Use the items in this list to write your own list. Put your most important need or want at the top and your least important need or want at the bottom. Then fill in the other things in order of importance to you. Compare your written list with a partner's. Discuss why you put things in that order.

Possible Things to Consider

Location (near work or bus line)

Cost of the housing

Size of the room or apartment

Safety features

Furnishings

Laundry facilities

Age of the housing

Ages of others who live there

Parking

Storage for bikes

My List

Most important to me:

_____

_____

_____

_____

_____

_____

_____

_____

Least important to me:

_____

B. What other things would you consider when choosing a place to live? Explain your answer.

_____

_____

_____

_____

Pacemaker® Skills for Independent Living   Copyright © by Pearson Education, Inc., publishing as Globe Fearon. All rights reserved.

An apartment rental agreement, or lease, is shown below. Study it and then answer the questions.

RENTAL AGREEMENT

Apple Apartments agrees to rent apartment __#24A__ to ___Jason Samuels___, who is referred to below as "the renter."

The rental period will begin on __July 1, 2001__ and continue until __June 30, 2002__. Apple Apartments or the renter may end this agreement by giving 30 days notice, in writing.

The renter agrees to pay a one-time security deposit of $500 and an additional $500 per month for each month of this agreement. Rent for each month must be paid by the first day of that month. Mail rent checks to Apple Apartments, 49 East Orange Road, Lansing, MI 48910.

The renter is responsible for electricity and telephone service. Apple Apartments will pay for water and garbage collection.

The renter must follow these rules:
1. Do not keep any pets in the apartment.
2. Do not paint the walls or ceilings.
3. To hang things on the walls, use hooks available in the rental office.
4. Make no loud noise, especially between 10:00 P.M. and 8:00 A.M.
5. Park only in your assigned spot.

_____   _____
Carrie Newsome   The renter
Apple Apartments Rental Agent

---

1. When is Jason's rent for August due?

_____

2. Suppose Jason gets a new job and must move to another city at the end of November. When should he tell Apple Apartments he is moving?

_____

3. Jason likes to take long, hot showers. Will his showers add to the cost of his apartment?

_____

4. What does Jason have to do if he wants to hang his baseball cap collection on the wall?

_____

Pacemaker® Skills for Independent Living   Copyright © by Pearson Education, Inc., publishing as Globe Fearon. All rights reserved.

19 ▸ Writing an Ad

Skill 19.3

Exercise 80

Critical Thinking

The McCabe family lives in a large house down the street from you. Last year, their oldest daughter moved out of the house and into her own apartment. She is doing well there, so the McCabes have decided to rent out her room.

Mrs. McCabe has asked for your help. She wants you to write a classified newspaper ad for the room. Begin by reviewing the classified ads in your newspaper. Keep your ad short and use some of the same abbreviations as in the newspaper ads. Be sure to tell readers how to contact Mrs. McCabe.

ROOM FOR RENT

_____

_____

_____

_____

_____

_____

Answer the questions below.

1. What part of your ad do you think readers will like? Why?

   _____

   _____

2. What are some things about a room for rent that are not likely to be included in an ad?

   _____

   _____

3. What has writing these ads taught you about reading real ads in the newspaper?

   _____

   _____

Pacemaker® Skills for Independent Living   Copyright © by Pearson Education, Inc., publishing as Globe Fearon. All rights reserved.

19 ▶ Living in a New Place   **Exercise 81**

Skills 19.4–19.5   *Critical Thinking*

Read the situations below. Then answer the questions.

1. Nina just signed the lease on her new apartment. She does not have any furniture except a bed. What else does she need? How could she get it?

   _____

   _____

   _____

2. Kenny is renting a room in a house with a community kitchen. His mom just got a new set of pans. What could he do with her old set of pans?

   _____

   _____

   _____

3. Mali and Denise share an apartment. What supplies do they need to keep their place neat? Why is it important to clean regularly?

   _____

   _____

   _____

4. Daniel never picks up after himself or cleans up his food messes. Do you think it is likely that he will get his security deposit back? Why or why not?

   _____

   _____

   _____

5. Lee is one week late paying this month's rent. Her car broke down, and she used her rent money to pay for repairs. She will be able to pay her landlord in three days when she gets her paycheck. In the meantime, she has not responded to messages left by her landlord. What is the best way to handle her situation?

   _____

   _____

   _____

Pacemaker® Skills for Independent Living   Copyright © by Pearson Education, Inc., publishing as Globe Fearon. All rights reserved.

20 ▶ Sorting Out Social Security   Exercise 82

Skill 20.1   *Critical Thinking*

Do you understand the purpose of your Social Security number?
Answer the questions below.

1. How many people have the same Social Security number that you do?
   Explain your answer.

   _____

   _____

   _____

2. When you apply for a Social Security card, what will you have to do?

   _____

   _____

   _____

3. Suppose you have a new job. However, you accidentally wrote the wrong Social
   Security number on your job application form. What problems will this cause?

   _____

   _____

   _____

4. What are some reasons you should not give your Social Security number to
   people who call you on the telephone?

   _____

   _____

   _____

5. When a woman gets married and changes her last name, does she need to apply
   for a new Social Security number? Explain your answer.

   _____

   _____

   _____

Pacemaker® Skills for Independent Living   Copyright © by Pearson Education, Inc., publishing as Globe Fearon. All rights reserved.

Name_____ Date_____

20 Understanding Voting

Exercise 83

Skill 20.2

Help these young adults become good citizens. Read each situation below and answer the questions.

1. It is August, and Nancy is going to the town library to register to vote. Her family is moving to another state in September. Nancy wants to register now so she can vote in the November elections.

   a. Will Nancy be able to vote in her new state in the November elections? Why or why not?

   _____

   _____

   _____

   b. What should Nancy do if she wants to vote in November?

   _____

   _____

   _____

2. It is almost time to elect a new mayor. John has heard one television commercial over and over. The commercial says that one candidate for mayor is going to raise everyone's taxes. John does not want to pay higher taxes. He decides to vote for the other candidate.

   a. Is John making a wise decision? Why or why not?

   _____

   _____

   _____

   b. What are some other things that John should find out before he votes?

   _____

   _____

   _____

Pacemaker® Skills for Independent Living Copyright © by Pearson Education, Inc., publishing as Globe Fearon. All rights reserved.

20 ▶ Writing a Letter to the Editor

Exercise 84

Skills 20.3, 20.5

Practice

You and a partner like to read the letters to the editor in your newspaper. Lately, several writers have complained about paying taxes and serving on juries.

In the space below, work with your partner to write a letter to the editor. Remind newspaper readers why people pay taxes and why they serve on juries. Explain what could happen if people did not do these things.

Dear Editor,

_____

_____

_____

_____

_____

_____

_____

_____

_____

_____

_____

_____

_____

_____

_____

_____

_____

_____

_____

Pacemaker® Skills for Independent Living   Copyright © by Pearson Education, Inc., publishing as Globe Fearon. All rights reserved.

20 ▶ Figuring Out Taxes   Exercise 85

Skills 20.3–20.4   *Critical Thinking*

You have been asked to help the people below do their taxes. Read each situation and answer the questions. Show your math.

1. Ned's W-2 form shows that he earned $13,500 last year and that his employer withheld $1,200 for federal income taxes. Ned figured out that he actually owes $1,065 in federal income tax. He decides to send the government a check for the difference between the two numbers: $135.

   a. What mistake is Ned making?

   _____

   _____

   b. What should Ned do about his taxes?

   _____

   _____

2. KC and her husband can file one tax form together, or they can each file a separate tax return. They each earned $17,000 this year. Here are the tax rates.

Tax Rate for Married Couples Who File a Tax Return Together	
15%	$0 to $43,850 in total income
28%	$43,850 to $105,950 in total income
Tax Rate for Married Couples Who File Separate Tax Returns	
15%	$0 to $21,925 each in income
28%	$21,925 to $52,975 each in income

   a. What is the tax rate for KC and her husband if they file a tax return together? What is the tax rate if they each file a separate return?

   _____

   _____

   b. If a married couple files separate tax returns, they each get a standard deduction of $4,300. If they file a tax return together, they get a standard deduction for a married couple of $7,200. Should KC and her husband file together or separately?

   _____

   _____

Pacemaker® Skills for Independent Living   Copyright © by Pearson Education, Inc., publishing as Globe Fearon. All rights reserved.

21 ▶ Writing a Letter of Advice **Exercise 86**

Skills 21.1–21.2 *Practice*

You have received the letter below from your friend Kia, who lives in another state.

Dear Friend,

I am so angry! I got my first speeding ticket today. The police officer said I was going 44 miles per hour, but the speed was 35 on that street. I was in a hurry to pick up my brother Robbie after his scout meeting. I was just trying to get there on time. Is that so terrible?

Why do the police care how fast you are driving anyway? I think you should be allowed to drive as fast as you think is safe. I know how good a driver I am, so I know how fast I can drive.

Now I have to pay a $100 fine. That is all the money I have. I hope this never happens to you.

Your friend,

Kia

Write Kia a letter. Show sympathy for her, but help her understand why drivers are not allowed to go as fast as they want to.

Dear Kia,

_____

_____

_____

_____

_____

_____

                                            _____

                                            _____

Pacemaker® Skills for Independent Living   Copyright © by Pearson Education, Inc., publishing as Globe Fearon. All rights reserved.

Name_____ Date_____

Skill 21.3   *Critical Thinking*

Laws for drivers, bike riders, and walkers are made to keep them and others safe. Schools and businesses also have rules to keep students and employees safe. Think of some school or business rules that are designed to keep you safe.

1. Write the rules in the chart below. Explain how each rule helps protect students or employees. Include rules you are asked to follow inside and outside your school or job.

Rule	How It Keeps You Safe

2. Share your rules with the class. List each one on the chalkboard.

3. Discuss the questions below as a class. Write important points on the lines.

   a. What kind of problems do the rules deal with? Why do you think that is so?

   _____

   _____

   b. Which rule do you think could be eliminated? Why?

   _____

   _____

   c. What new rule would you add? Why?

   _____

   _____

Pacemaker® Skills for Independent Living   Copyright © by Pearson Education, Inc., publishing as Globe Fearon. All rights reserved.

21 ▶ Designing a Poster

Exercise 88

Skills 21.2–21.4

Practice

A. Choose a law that is often violated in your community. You could call your police department and ask which laws are violated most often. Do not call 911 to ask. Use the non-emergency number listed in the phone book.

Then design a poster in the space below to encourage people to obey the law you chose. The poster needs to convince people that laws protect them in some way.

B. Answer the questions below.

1. What kinds of accidents and injuries do laws help prevent?

_____

_____

2. What are some reasons people disobey laws?

_____

_____

3. Do laws take away people's rights? If so, is this fair?

_____

_____

Pacemaker® Skills for Independent Living   Copyright © by Pearson Education, Inc., publishing as Globe Fearon. All rights reserved.

Name _____   Date _____

21 ▶ Making a Map

Skills 21.1, 21.3

Exercise 89

Complete the following activities.

1. Draw a map of the way you would walk, ride a bike, or drive a car from your home to school or work. Include the names of streets and landmarks.

N
W ◄ ◆ ► E
S

2. Suppose your community had no traffic laws, traffic signs, or traffic lights. Describe four problems you would face on your way to your destination. Use your map to explain where the problems would occur.

a. Problem: _____

_____

b. Problem: _____

_____

c. Problem: _____

_____

d. Problem: _____

_____

Pacemaker® Skills for Independent Living   Copyright © by Pearson Education, Inc., publishing as Globe Fearon. All rights reserved.

Name_____ Date_____

Go on a "Help Hunt." Use a phone book to identify agencies that could
help with the problems below. Fill in your answers on the lines.

Problems:

1. I think I should be getting unemployment checks, but I am not sure.

   Agency: _____   Phone Number: _____

2. My water bill is much higher than usual this month.

   Agency: _____   Phone Number: _____

3. I need a passport.

   Agency: _____   Phone Number: _____

4. I have a question about my federal income tax.

   Agency: _____   Phone Number: _____

5. I would like to find some interesting activities for my grandfather.

   Agency: _____   Phone Number: _____

6. I want to join the Army.

   Agency: _____   Phone Number: _____

7. My neighbor's welfare check is late, and I want to help him.

   Agency: _____   Phone Number: _____

8. My brother wants to get a marriage license.

   Agency: _____   Phone Number: _____

9. My grandmother's Social Security check is late.

   Agency: _____   Phone Number: _____

10. I want to talk to my U.S. Senator.

    Agency: _____   Phone Number: _____

Pacemaker® Skills for Independent Living   Copyright © by Pearson Education, Inc., publishing as Globe Fearon. All rights reserved.

Name_____   Date_____

22 ▶ Relaying Messages   Exercise 91

Skill 22.3   *Critical Thinking*

A. Work with two other people to try out a message relay service.
   Follow the steps below. Two people in the group will send messages
   back and forth with the help of the third "relay" person. The relay
   person will be the only one who talks.

   STEP 1   The first person will write a message.

   STEP 2   The relay person will read that message aloud to the third person.

   STEP 3   The third person will write a response.

   STEP 4   The relay person will read the third person's response aloud to the first person.

B. After trying out the relay service, answer these questions.

   1. What kinds of communication problems would the relay service help with?

   _____

   _____

   _____

   2. What problems did you have in using the service? What are some ways to overcome
      these problems?

   _____

   _____

   _____

   3. How is a relay service similar to computer e-mail? How is it different?

   _____

   _____

   _____

   4. Do you think a person who works for a relay service needs to be patient? How about
      the person who needs to use the service? Explain your answers.

   _____

   _____

   _____

Pacemaker® Skills for Independent Living   Copyright © by Pearson Education, Inc., publishing as Globe Fearon. All rights reserved.

22 ▶ Researching Community Activities   Exercise 92

Skill 22.4   *Critical Thinking*

A. List three activities in your community that each group below might
enjoy. Choose activities that are open to the public and inexpensive or
free. Begin by listing activities you know about. Then add to your lists
by checking the newspaper or your community recreation department.

Preschoolers (infants to age 4):

1. _____

2. _____

3. _____

Elementary School Children (ages 5–12):

1. _____

2. _____

3. _____

Teenagers (ages 13–19):

1. _____

2. _____

3. _____

Single Adults (ages 20–35):

1. _____

2. _____

3. _____

B. Answer these questions.

1. Which activities on the lists are well-known and well-attended? Why is that?

_____

2. Which group has the least activities available, as far as you know? Do you think
this causes problems for that group? Why or why not?

_____

Pacemaker® Skills for Independent Living   Copyright © by Pearson Education, Inc., publishing as Globe Fearon. All rights reserved.